Dear Claire,

A Story For Megan To Aspire To.

Congratulations....

Love
Charlie.

For Ydora Wredge

Once upon a time there was a baby.

It was worse than other babies. For one thing, it was larger.

Its body was not merely obese, but downright bloated.

One of its feet had too many toes,
and the other one not enough.

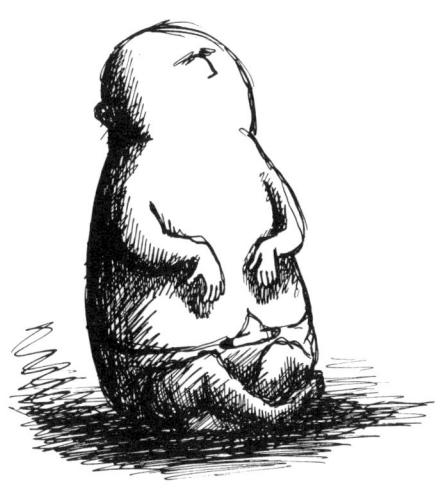

Its hands were both left ones.

Its nose was beaky, and appeared to be considerably older than the rest of it.

Its tiny eyes were surrounded by large black rings due to fatigue, for its guilty conscience hardly <u>ever</u> allowed it to sleep.

It was usually damp and sticky for it wept a great deal. It was consumed by self-pity, which in this case was perfectly justified.

It was capable of making only two sorts of noises, both of them nasty.

The first was a choked gurgling, reminiscent of faulty drains. It made this noise when it had succeeded in doing something particularly atrocious.

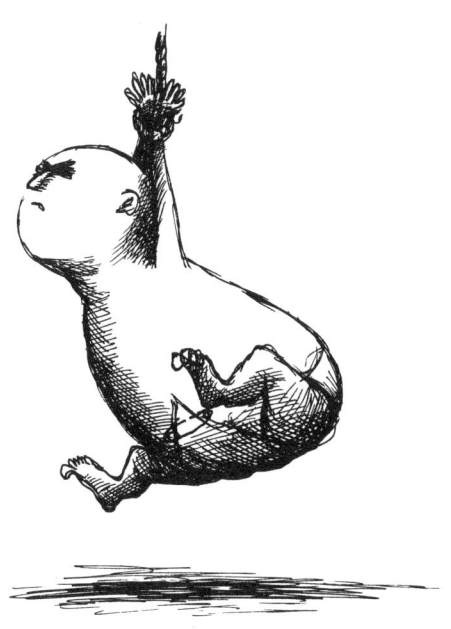

The second was a thin shriek suggestive of fingernails on blackboards. It made this noise when it had been prevented from doing something particularly atrocious.

Fortunately, it was unable to walk.

It had never been given a name since no-one cared to talk about it. When it was absolutely necessary to do so, it was referred to as the Beastly Baby.

Dangerous objects were left about in the hope that it would do itself an injury, preferably fatal.

But it never did, and instead, hacked up the carpets with knives.

Or burnt enormous holes in the upholstery with acid.

Or shot bric-à-brac off the tables.

A day in the broiling sun had no other effect than to turn it a horrid purple.

When it was taken bathing, it always floated back to shore, festooned with slimy green weed.

In public places some officious person was certain to point out that it was in danger of being left behind.

Inevitably, a policeman was looking on whenever it was just about to be momentarily set down on a doorstep.

In the meantime it grew larger and older every day, and what this would eventually lead to, no-one liked to think.

Then one day it was taken on a picnic.

It was set on an exposed ledge some distance from where the food was.

A few minutes later, a passing eagle noticed it there.

The eagle, having never before been presented with this classic opportunity, carried it off.

The eagle found keeping hold of it more difficult than he had expected.

He attempted to get a further grip on it with his beak.

There was a wet sort of explosion, audible for several miles.

And <u>that</u>, thank heavens! was the end of the Beastly Baby.